Password Tracker

Website	User Name	Password

I0475370

Password Tracker

Website	User Name	Password

Password Tracker

Website	User Name	Password

Password Tracker

Website	User Name	Password

Password Tracker

Website	User Name	Password

Password Tracker

Website	User Name	Password

Password Tracker

Website	User Name	Password

Password Tracker

Website	User Name	Password

Password Tracker

Website	User Name	Password

Password Tracker

Website	User Name	Password

Password Tracker

Website	User Name	Password

Password Tracker

Website	User Name	Password

Password Tracker

Website	User Name	Password

Password Tracker

Website	User Name	Password

Password Tracker

Website	User Name	Password

Password Tracker

Website	User Name	Password

Password Tracker

Website	User Name	Password

Password Tracker

Website	User Name	Password

Password Tracker

Website	User Name	Password

Password Tracker

Website	User Name	Password

Password Tracker

Website	User Name	Password

Password Tracker

Website	User Name	Password

www.ingramcontent.com/pod-product-compliance
Lightning Source LLC
Chambersburg PA
CBHW071727170526
45165CB00005B/2186